STATIUS: SII

Poetry by *Anthony Howell*

Inside the Castle   1969

Imruil   1970

Oslo: a Tantric Ode   1975

Notions of a Mirror   1983

Why I May Never See the Walls of China   1986

Howell's Law   1990

First Time in Japan   1995

Sonnets   1999

Selected Poems   2000

Spending   2000

Dancers in Daylight   2003

Poetry by *Bill Shepherd*

Sun, Oak, Almond I   1970

Evidences   1980

Self-Love   1983

Horace: The Complete Odes and Epodes   1983

Propertius: The Poems   1986

Mother's Milk   2006

Statius: *Silvae*

A SELECTION

VERSIONS BY

Anthony Howell
and
Bill Shepherd

ANVIL PRESS POETRY

Published in Great Britain in 2007
by Anvil Press Poetry Ltd
Neptune House   70 Royal Hill   London   SE10 8RF
www.anvilpresspoetry.com

This book is published with financial assistance
from Arts Council England

Set in Monotype Fournier
Printed and bound in England
by Cromwell Press, Trowbridge, Wiltshire

ISBN 978 0 85646 387 7

ACKNOWLEDGEMENT

The version from Statius ("Siluae 5.4: On Sleep") on page 95 is from
The Poems of J. V. Cunningham, edited with an Introduction
and Commentary by Tim Steele, 1997. Reprinted with permission
of Swallow Press / Ohio University Press, Athens, Ohio
(www.ohioswallow.com)

CONTENTS

Book V

APPENDIX

SONNET IX

Sleep, Silence' child, sweet father of soft rest,
Prince, whose approach peace to all mortals brings,
Indifferent host to shepherds and to kings,
Sole comforter of minds with grief opprest;
Lo, by thy charming rod all breathing things
Lie slumb'ring, with forgetfulness possest,
And yet o'er me to spread thy drowsy wings
Thou spares, alas! who cannot be thy guest.
Since I am thine, O come, but with that face
To inward light which thou art wont to show,
With feigned solace ease a true-felt woe;
Or if, deaf god, thou do deny that grace,
Come as thou wilt, and what thou wilt bequeath,
I long to kiss the image of my death.

DRUMMOND OF HAWTHORNDEN

INTRODUCTION

Publius Papinius Statius was the foremost exponent of occasional verse in the Silver Age of Latin poetry. Each of his *Silvae* address a particular event, such as the inauguration of a newly built swimming-pool or the completion of a major road. Often Statius has a particular patron in mind, for instance, the owner of the villa where the swimming-pool is being installed, or the emperor who has decreed that the new road should come into existence. Detractors might accuse the poet of being the first spin-doctor – putting a favourable gloss on some official announcement – maybe folk were grumbling about how much the road had cost. He could certainly spin things out. Where Martial, his contemporary, prided himself on his brevity and refined the terse and pithy *epigram*, Statius favoured the *encomium*, which makes a virtue out of discursiveness. His ode to the Via Domitiana is nearly as long as the road itself.

He asserts that he extemporized, being more than willing to declaim, when moved to do so, during the event in question, and jotting the poem down, with few alterations, over the next few days. This makes him something of a "performance poet". He was probably born in the AD 50s, a decade or two after the death of Christ. But whereas Christ was the instigator of deceptively simple but deep pronouncements such as "Love thy neighbour" and "Turn the other cheek" – pronouncements that sound appropriately archaic – Statius's writing reminds one of features for *House and Garden*. His descriptions have an almost photographic accuracy about them and constitute a unique source of information for architectural historians researching into the building techniques and design that characterized his day. His style is gushing and he knows how to chat, or, rather, how to chatter.

He was the son of a scholar-knight who had lost his equestrian status, possibly because his studies in religious lore had led him to neglect matters of finance, though he did tutor the emperor in this

9

esoteric subject. Papinius Senior was also a professional poet who had distinguished himself in several minor competitions, in Greek more often than in Roman verse. The family were of Greek origin, from South Italy, and Statius considered Naples and its vicinity (Capua and Puteoli) to be his true *heimat*, and indeed he retired there towards the end of his life. Then as now, the careers of poets were advanced by competitions, though the adjudication of these was focussed on live performances rather than on submissions.

In his father's lifetime, Statius won at the Augustalia, which was held in Naples, as had his father before him. The high point came when he won at the Alban Games, reciting to a circle of courtiers and to the Emperor himself, in the amphitheatre above the crater which contains Lake Albano – "the Mirror of Diana". This magical little amphitheatre can be found in the gardens of Domitian's summer palace in the Alban hills, a few miles from Rome. It is now the Pope's summer residence. Domitian pronounced himself the high priest of his own divinity, and the Pope is still "Princeps" – as were the emperors of old.

Statius married Claudia, the widow of a poet (it is not known who he was). She had one daughter and appears to have supplied her second husband with her own ambitious drive while still promoting the work of her first. In his heyday, Statius owned a small estate at Alba Longa, equipped by Domitian with a water supply – an estate which may actually have been a gift from the Emperor to his father. He completed one epic – the *Thebaid* – embarked on another, and, being strapped for cash, according to Juvenal, he composed the libretto for a piece to be performed by Paris, the greatest mime ever seen in Rome. But then things began to look less rosy. Domitian had ordered the assassination of Paris in 83 for carrying on an affair with his wife Domitia, from whom he had separated (in order to have a fling with his niece Julia), only to demand a reconciliation with Domitia after Julia had died while having an abortion. Paris was the loser in this imbroglio, and any friend of Paris might well have felt uncomfortable in Rome after his death. Statius failed to win the Capitoline Games, the most coveted award of the epoch, some time after this. He attended banquets given by the Emperor, but at one infamous banquet a funerary atmosphere prevailed and the guests dined off their tombstones. A reign of terror had begun. Statius completed the last two books of his *Silvae* from the comparative safety of the Neapolitan hinterland.

As well as meaning "a wood", *silva* can mean matter, and may denote undergrowth as well as trees. The phrase "raw material" comes to mind, and indicates unworked or improvised expression. There is something here of the minstrel in *Asterix* who usually gets gagged and tied to a tree at feasts. The suggestion of "non-finito" may of course be a pose – "oh, it's just a little something I tossed off the other day!" Much of the material seems highly wrought by contemporary standards, though there are some bizarre shifts of tense and instances of scrambled metaphor that may point to rushed construction. *Silva* also suggests a miscellany, as Ben Jonson used *The Forrest* for a heterogeneous collection of odes, epistles and songs, and as Robert Louis Stevenson subsequently used *Underwoods* – also to describe an assortment of literary pieces.

The subjects Statius deals with include an equestrian statue of Domitian, the locks of the Emperor's favourite eunuch (later Domitian prohibited castration), and an imperial banquet. Statius has been decried as the greatest toady ever to have spouted. D. A. Slater, writing an introduction to the *Silvae* in 1908, goes so far as to maintain that it would have been better for the poet's reputation if time had buried the seven "court poems", written by Statius "with a view to his advancement in high places." There is however something neatly ironical about the praise he lavishes on the tyrant to whom he was the laureate. David Salle, the American artist, has said of the films of Douglas Sirk that they so extravagantly endorse the dynastic environment of their characters – oil magnates, playboys, tycoons – that they satirize by exaggeration. Burgeoning grandeur subverts its vaunted intent and proves deflationary. Statius works the same double-take, I feel, and it's a view shared by A. J. Boyle in his Penguin introduction to the *Silvae*:

"... deft in its control of nuance and hyperbole – and more complex in the demands it makes of its readers – is the encomium on Domitian (IV.2), a text that has been seriously misread. Many still find evidence in this poem for the conventional view of Statius as imperial bootlicker. The poem is in fact a paradigm of ironic eulogy. From Virgil onwards imperial panegyric was a necessary and complex discourse more often defined by latent, critical irony than self-seeking adulation: the mode of double-speak in an age of tyranny. The poet who indicted the abuse of monarchial power in the *Thebaid* was under no illusions about Domitian."

Roman Poets of the Early Empire (Penguin Classics, 1991) ed. A. J. Boyle and J. P. Sullivan, p. 221.

Other subjects are less fraught with danger. These are addressed to patrons who were clearly friends. There's a poem to Melior's parrot, another on a cheap book received as a gift, and one on a lavish wedding. The *Silvae* are characterized by ingenious thought-processes and some reveal deep feeling – as we find in the poem to his deceased father or in the one to his wife, exhorting her to leave Rome. They also exhibit an astute sense of how to use detail to conjure forth an image, while the poet's ability to control the forms he employs is never less than impeccable. Admittedly, he is a mannerist – the restrictions on content demanded by an autocratic *imperium* obliged Statius to work in this vein. Ernst Robert Curtius provides us with a definitive characterization of what it means:

"The mannerist wants to say things not normally but abnormally. He prefers the artificial and the affected to the natural. He wants to surprise, to astonish, to dazzle. While there is only one way of saying things naturally, there are a thousand forms of unnaturalness."

European Literature and the Latin Middle Ages (Bern, 1948) trans. W. R. Trask, London 1953, p. 282.

The capricious extravagance of mannerism is a strategy for escaping from the doldrums of a standard classicism that tends to be the legacy of any "Golden Age" (in this case that of Virgil and Horace, a century before). And where the mannered style concerns stanza-form in the poetry of another empire – I'm thinking of Swinburne in the Victorian age – for Statius it concerns a capacity to exaggerate the figures of rhetoric. He rises above the prevailing orthodoxy by the sheer number of classical allusions he can pile on, usually with a fair degree of wit. He can also imbue a trivial event with an epic mythology. But this gives him a handle on the ordinary. So, ironically enough, the mannerism that gives him such a stylish style also opens the door to a species of naturalism, for in fact he is one of the first poets to describe the humble and mundane occurrences of everyday life – the gift of a book, the shape of a tree in a garden.

BILL SHEPHERD and I share an appreciation of this poet but our methods of translating him occupy different ends of the spectrum. His own grasp of Latin is excellent, and his translations are accurate and well researched. Also, because he is a fine poet, they are evidently poems in their own right, informed by an aware ear and a confident grasp on scansion and form that does justice to the originals. Rather than translations, my own attempts may be better referred to as versions or imitations. My Latin is less than rudimentary, despite years of learning the declensions in various abysmal class-rooms. I make poems from these *Silvae* in order to appreciate them, since I cannot really get to their original felicities. I work from whatever cribs I can get hold of, read "between the lines" and try to make the best poetry I can out of clusters of words that veil as much as they disclose. I work at that which inspires me in any poem, and sometimes abandon my attempt before getting to the actual conclusion. Some of the poems I have had a go at have also been translated by Bill, and there are others neither of us have found a way into, so this is by no means a thorough or comprehensive rendition of the *Silvae* into English. However, it does represent a homage by two poets to one whose work remains relevant nearly two thousand years after his death. Or maybe it's his irrelevance that we appreciate. His work is not informed by the satirical savagery that we know from Juvenal, he lacks the salacious obscenity of Martial, and he is not a consummate story teller like Ovid. But for Dante he was "il dolce poeta", and he has his place in Chaucer's *House of Fame*. He has a certain grace. It's a matter of elegance, and of diffidence. The classical parallels are piled on in accordance with rhetorical theory and its demand for high-flown examples of similar mythological occurrences. We get great lists of them, yet they are delivered with a self-deprecation that belies belief in the system purportedly being promoted. Statius has a non-heroic view of himself. This enables him to become his own anti-hero, an anxious man who whinges sometimes, and attempts to list his successes while he can't help but call to mind his disappointments. At the court of someone a bit like Saddam, he is trying not to put a foot wrong, and suffering from insomnia in the process. The tone of his voice can sound distinctly modern.

ANTHONY HOWELL
February 2003

ADDENDUM TO THE INTRODUCTION

This addendum is primarily a gloss on the "excellent" Latin and "careful research" with which Anthony Howell credits me. I offer it because I am interested in the mysterious psychospiritual and transpersonal processes which some translators, including myself, seem to experience.

There have been three main tranches in my translation of Latin poetry, the odes and epodes of Horace, all the extant poetry of Propertius, and the selection of Statius's *Silvae* included in this book. At the outset of each project I evoked and invoked within myself the presence of the relevant poet, asking him to enable me to serve his poetry as well as I could. The poet seemed to respond, and thereafter I was *obsessed* with the project until it was finished. At every possible opportunity I would take to my bed with the Latin text, the Loeb crib, a Latin-English dictionary (for Horace this was the *Teach Yourself Latin* paperback dictionary), one or two reference books and/or previous translations.

My only formal qualification in Latin is an "A" level obtained in 1952, after which I didn't look at a single line of Latin until I set myself to translate about 1975 a few fragments attributed to Petronius. In bed with Horace, Propertius or Statius, I found the translationese of Loeb so cloudily imprecise as to be almost meaningless, but the crib did explicate for me the grammatical and syntactical structure of the next sentence, and the next, and the next. Endlessly thumbing the dictionary and interrogating memory, high on a rush of bright ideas, I advanced a line at a time. Like an archaeologist meticulously unearthing a Roman mosaic floor, I painstakingly *revealed to myself*, almost in its final form, my own new poem-translation.

Except that it was mine only in a particular sense. Repeatedly it felt as though, or I experienced the reality that, the poem-translation emerged through, rather than originated within, me. Again and again I was reminded of the Zen archer: I did not "make these translations" in the usual sense of the words; rather, it seemed that I was the participant (albeit a necessary one) in a transpersonal process that occurred. I enjoyed a sense of wonder and privilege that this was so – unlike the archer, I had done nothing to earn this experience of connectedness.

For the duration of each project I enjoyed a dream-like sense of empowerment. For example, at a time when I had read Ezra Pound's *Homage to Sextus Propertius* but only *one line* of the poet himself, I offered confidently to "do Propertius". In retrospect this looks like foolhardy arrogance, yet it was a serious suggestion eventually taken up by Penguin, and today "my Propertius" is a book I stand by.

In his *Statian Addresses* (as he has called them) Anthony Howell writes "creative translation" – a term adopted by J. P. Sullivan to describe Pound's *Homage*. His versions are poems "after" his author, or "imitations", his illustrious forebears in this genre including the Pound of the *Homage* and even the Pope of *Imitations of Horace*. He tries to see for himself, in his own *persona* and style, what Statius sees. I try to see through Statius's Roman eyes what Statius sees, adopting a diction and style which are the result of imagining that English was the language of Rome. I try at once to translate line for line, imitating Statius's counterpoint of syntactic lay-out against lineation, and to arrive at an outcome which is a poem.

For this present book I have made some amendments to the text included in the anthology *Roman Poets of the Early Empire*, edited by A. J. Boyle and J. P. Sullivan (Penguin, 1991) and have added new translations of II.4, "Melior's Parrot" and IV.5, "Ode to Septimus Severus."

Finally, I would like to say a few words about each of the *Silvae* poems I have translated.

The First of December (I.6)

Straightforward description and evocation of an evening of appalling fun at the Colosseum. Some of the details of the entertainment adumbrate feasible future series of our own "reality TV" shows: the "housemates" in *Big Brother* and/or the "celebs" in *I'm a Celebrity ... Get Me Out of Here!* will be obliged, without any instruction or previous experience, to engage in armed combat, then rewarded or consoled by having oven-ready flamingoes and pheasants dropped on their heads.

Melior's Parrot (II.4)

Written in a style readers of English Augustan verse will recognize as mock-heroic, this at one level a witty pastiche of Statius' own *epicedia* (commemorative poems praising the lives of dead persons – see V.3 below).

The hyperbolic praise here seems to me to mock the parrot, yet sharply observed details of description suggest a genuine fondness. And there is for me a curious pathos in the thought that the lot of this bird in a silver cage, imprisoned by and required to entertain beings so much more powerful than himself, is not totally dissimilar to that of a career-poet in Domitian's Rome.

Thanksgiving to the Emperor Augustus Germanicus Domitianus (IV.2)

Disallow the view (expressed in Anthony Howell's introduction) that the flattery is ironic and satirical, and this piece is an almost unbearable instance of self-humiliation; allow it (as I must), and the poem is a lively and brave *tour de force*.

Ode to Septimius Severus (IV.5)

This tentative venture into Alcaic metre is fairly routine as to content, but the style is enlivened by touches of the mannerism which Anthony Howell addresses. I have tried to match instances of mannered diction while sticking fairly close to the literal meaning of the Latin. Thus

> *non mille balant lanigeri greges,*
> *nec vacca dulci mugit adultero,*

for example, becomes

> No woolly thousands bleat,
> No cow moos for her paramour . . .

Jocular Lines to Plotius Grypus (IV.9)

Grypus' book-for-a-book joke is a subject on which Martial or Catullus might have written a scathing epigram of some six or eight lines: Statius spins out the occasion over fifty lines of hendecasyllables. And where Martial or Catullus would have written with animus, Statius' poem, as it runs through its absurd lists, transmits a genial good humour which I find very attractive. "'I'm angry with you, Grypus' – but only a little bit."

In Memory of My Father (V.3)

The diction is formal, the syntax complex and the style densely allusive to mythological and (to a lesser extent) historical persons and events. There is no overall unfolding of a narrative, descriptive or discursive process. For these reasons the poem seemed, when I first read it, to mark time, or to proceed only at the rate of a glacier. Then I saw that the piece is a *monument* made of words, a memorial. A memorial is stationary. There it is, on the church wall: it doesn't move.

Statius says (lines 47–50):

> I wish it were my lot to tender an altar to your shade,
> A work matching temples – to raise an airy fabric
> Higher than Cyclopes' crags, or pyramids' daring masonry,
> And to border your mound with a large grove!

This is not literally possible, but he performs the equivalent in literary terms, creating a truly imposing (293 lines) *tombeau* of more-than-Baroque elaboration and grandeur – a vehicle adaptable enough to enable Statius to address his father not just in the language of laudatory inscription, but also (fairly consistently in the final sixty or so lines) in that of personal feeling.

To Sleep (V.4)

The most accessible and popular of Statius' poems. As others have noted, one can relate to it readily as a sort of nineteen-line blank sonnet to sleep.

BILL SHEPHERD
December 2005

THE DEDICATION OF THE SWIMMING POOL

O Hippocrene, your chill source on Helicon
Is actually too sober for my present strain,
And far too often have the weary muses
Scratched their heads to find me happy uses.
Phoebus will not do, since he'll have sunk,
While Bacchus gets so nasty when he's drunk,
And everyone would find it too mechanical
If I should call on Hermes with his tortoise-shell.
My poem must rely upon some other set:
Lovely girls emerging from the water-jet,
And Vulcan, coming reddened out of Etna
With every smith, from Timbuctoo to Gretna,
Who ever felt that he could use a bath.
My own ongoing epic on the wrath
That shook the town of Thebes is inappropriate:
I need a lighter touch if I'm to dedicate
This swimming-pool with some degree of flair,
Which is of course the reason why I'm here.
Tilt the jug more, don't be such a kill-joy,
Tilt again, and let me drink my fill, boy.
Loose the heavy toga of dull care,
And I'll proclaim this pool beyond compare:
A place of gleaming stone and dazzling water
Whose muse is young enough to be my daughter.
Wound about with ribbons and with ivy,
She makes Etruscus feel distinctly divey
When she saunters in without a fig-leaf
To splash him till he has her by the midriff.

Goddesses of ocean, turn away
From riding dolphins on the open sea.
Your salty hair's been blown awry by blusters:
Fix it up with ivy-berry clusters
And glide towards us, wearing not a stitch,
Just as when you make the satyrs itch
By deep inlets. Not that I would hail
Those of you who've left a lurid trail
Behind you as you gaily cleave the wave:
I'm going to ban Salmacis for her treachery,
Who'd have our lads effeminized by lechery;
While that Oenone should be kept in wraps,
Whose fountain's dry since love turned off the taps;
And Dryope had better be prohibited,
Who told poor Hylas not to feel inhibited.
I wouldn't want it said that our young men
Were here one day then never seen again.
Instead, I'll send a cordial invitation
To each naiad of our Latin nation:
No less fluid, more to be relied on;
Those who use the Tiber's flood to ride on;
Those who, with the Anio, choose to go
Plunging into virgin pools below,
And others welling from the Marsian snow:
Their services are welcomed by my song
Because their pressing ripples bowl along
The airy ducts above our countless arches,
Eager to ensure no Roman parches.
Nymphs with magisterial abilities,
Sylphs aware of state responsibilities,
Sprites who never dawdle in their tracks

Need upon occasion to relax:
Rest assured, girls, here we'll get you blotto:
All the guides rate this a five-star grotto.
Venus even took her husband's hand
And guided it to where it might command
A fiercer warmth, exhorting him to stoke
His furnaces with flaming hearts for coke,
And used the torches of her chubby acolytes
To ignite the votive flames and pilot-lights.
Here the marble quarried out of Thasos
Has no place, nor Carystine asbestos,
Nor its cipolino; there's no call
For onyx, and no snake-stone used at all.
Here instead we find a gleaming brown
Porphyry from Algiers, and milky stone
Flecked with drops of Attis' blood from caves
King Midas mined with his Synnadic slaves.
The architraves are of a deeper hue
Than linen dyed at Tyre: they're almost blue,
And interrupt that dado of Sage Derby
Picking out the marble from the porphyry.
Floors and ceilings shine, while Aesop's fables
Crowd the stained-glass windows in the gables.
Furthermore, the altar-fire appears
Impressed by this magnificence and swears
It knows its duty is to fit the bill:
It's not a bonfire, it's a charcoal-grill
Whose embers fail to glow when it's so bright
On every side the dazzle hurts the sight.
Indeed the sun pours in with all his might
And burns himself upon these baking stones.

Luxurious? I swear the only bronze
You'll find is on those girls without bikinis
Putting oil on Claudius's penis.
Water pours from silver into silver,
Laughs and gurgles, or delays its rill there,
Poised upon the brink as if it gazed
Into its own loveliness, amazed
At what it saw and loathe to quit the pool.
Through the columns, I can see the cool
River's blueness, twinkling in its reaches,
Where it touches incandescent beaches,
Unpolluted, and without an undertow:
Who would not be tempted to undo
His interfering togs and take dip?
Cytherea should have been washed up
Against these shores: Narcissus might have clipped
His image here: Diana would have stripped,
Hardly caring whether someone saw her.
Now however we should try the sauna.
I believe its temperature's built up
Since I can hear the ventilator's flap
Inviting us to lounge around and sweat,
Or even try a damper sort of heat.
A visitor from any swank resort
You care to name would never dare to snort
At what's been laid on here for private use,
And no one could aver that I abuse
The Baths of Nero, larger though they are,
By saying someone hotfoot from that spa
Might be prepared to do it over here.
Claudius Etruscus, your relations

And your friends extend congratulations:
We admire your taste, your ingenuity,
And wish your baths and you a perpetuity
Of noble banquets and successful chases
Round the poolside. May the blessed graces
All combine to celebrate your nights
And urge your rocket on to greater heights.

[A. H.]

THE FIRST OF DECEMBER

Go, keep holiday far away,
Father Apollo, stern Pallas, you Muses:
We'll call you back on January first.
Saturn, your fetters all unloosed,
December, loaded with copious wine,
And laughing Mirth and salty Wit –
To me! I'll report the happy feast
Of cheerful Caesar's vinous peace.

Scarce had Aurora stirred new day,
Already sweetmeats rained from the rope –
Such the dews the east wind lavished.
The much-loved nuts from Pontic groves,
Dates from Idume's fertile heights,
Damsons that budded in godly Damascus,
And figs that Parching Caunus ripened,
Fall without payment – plentiful plunder;
Biscuits and melting gingerbread men,
Amerian apples and pears just ripe,
And laurel cakes, and swelling dates
From bowered palms were showered down.
The Hyades and melted Pleiads
Don't swamp the earth with troubling storms
As winter "hail" from sunny skies
Then crushed the Roman theatre's throng.
Let Jupiter marshal clouds around the world,
And menace with storms the widespread fields,
While our Roman Jove brings showers like these!

But see – another group that looks
Well-dressed, distinctive, no less than those
Already seated, threads the throng.
These are carrying baskets of bread,
Dazzling napkins, and richer food;
Those pour out lavishly drowsy wine –
You'd think each one an Idaean waiter.
Since, prosperous Sir, you feast the rows
Of those of the senior, graver sort,
Proud Price knows nothing of this day.
Antiquity, go, compare these times
With the age of gold, of primeval Jove:
Wine did not flow so freely then,
Nor harvest pre-empt the tardy year.
One table feeds all ranks, children,
Women, senators, commons, knights:
Freedom remits respect of degree.
Indeed, even You – what god could find
Such leisure, vouchsafe so much? –
Attended with us the general banquet.
So now the poor, the rich – whoever –
Glory in being the Emperor's guests.

Amidst the din and novel confusion
The pleasure of watching flies lightly by:
Untrained swordswomen take their stand,
Commence sub-standard mannish fights –
You'd think that Amazon platoons
Sweated by Don or outlandish Phasis.
Here swarms a bold array of dwarfs
Whose natural growth, abruptly stopped,

Has bound them for good in knotty lumps.
They deal out wounds in hand to hand fight
And threaten death – and with what fists!
Bloody Manhood and father Mars both laugh,
And cranes hovering for scattered spoils
Are aghast at these most dauntless thugs.
Now as the shades of night draw on,
Uproar keeps flowing what largess!
Enter girls (reasonably priced)!
We find here all that on the stage
Is praised for skill and pleases by looks.
Plump Lydian girls in a gaggle clap,
There Spanish cymbals jingle and clash,
There Syrians chatter together in droves,
And here show-business' lower orders,
And traders of matches for broken glass.
Amidst which suddenly drop from the sky
Innumerable birds – flamingoes – from Nile,
Phasis pheasants, and guinea fowl culled
By Numidians in the humid south.
Captors lack: all here are glad to fill
Their tunics, adding still fresh winnings.
Countless voices are raised to heaven
Extolling the Emperor's festive day,
Acclaiming their "Lord" with warm goodwill –
But this one liberty He banned.

Dusk was just overwhelming the world,
When into the arena's thickest shade
Ball-lightning fell, surpassing the glitter
Of Ariadne's constellation.

The Pole shone out in fire, and allowed
Lawful nothing of darkling night.
Sluggish Rest fled – and indolent Sleep,
Seeing this, went off to other cities.
Who can sing the licensed mirth,
Social bond, the feasting free of cost,
And generous Lyaeus' streams of wine?
Bacchus, I wilt beneath you now,
And drag myself, late and drunk, to bed.

This annual feast shall always continue –
No age shall ever see it decay!
While father Tiber, the Latian hills,
And while Your Rome, and the Capitol You
Have restored, shall stand, it shall remain.

[B. S.]

A DAY AT THE CIRCUS

We can't count on decent weather, dears.
The *ancien regime* is not invited,
Austerity will see her measures flouted,
And as for our nine solemn dowagers,
They've been sent to winter in the south.
The old cats – wish them a good riddance!
Let's unbind the olive-rooted claws
Of rustic Saturn, god of winter storage:
He and dark December like to celebrate
With as many skins as they can flatten.
Filch me a handful of quips, a bushel of cringe;
Then if you will vouchsafe to sit with me,
I'll come up with some impromptu lay
In honour of the merry little geezer
Putting up the money for this binge.

Scarcely had we rubbed our eyes today,
Than lollipops came raining from the awnings:
Manna out of heaven, you might say.
Surely a hurricane must have accosted
The nut-groves of Pontus, surely the vines
Reserved for Bacchus must have been
Ransacked on Edom. Every decent damson
From Damascus, Ebusean fig and tangerine
Showering down from the upstairs boxes:
When before has waste been so conspicuous?
Honeyed cakes, treats to set you drooling,

Bitable pears from Ameria, not the sort
Made squidgy in the market by the sun,
And so many dates to a cluster, dears.
You'd never get down to the stem.
Munificence rather darkened the air.
Would the gale-wracked Hyades,
Could the flummoxed Pleiades provide
A fury like this amicable hail
Of edible missiles fired on the people
Crowded into the theatre there?
Jupiter may roll about as drastically
As any gothic god upon his cumulus,
Menacing the vista with his thunderbolts,
Just so long as Jupiter on earth
Can still afford this tempest once a year.

Look at them, look at the toffs!
Wafted in from fashion mags,
I think they must have washed before
They gathered on their balconies
To smile at us. Do my eyes deceive me:
Are there as many of them up there
As there are of us folk on the benches?
Languidly they lean from balustrades,
Tipping up platters, pelting us with
Doughnuts. How dazzling the napkins
From which they now unleash
A second batch! Torrents of befuddlement
Are offered by the smarter set:
You might suppose each gilded youth a Ganymede.

Banquet equally, Oh Lord and Master,
Charmed circles, pundits, legal eagles,
Using up your precious private income
To snub Annona, mistress of the dole.
Don't begin to shake your head, old gaffer:
It's presumptuous to compare today
With that gauche age mistook for Golden.
Honest to god, you never had it so good.
When did you get vino gratis, eh?
When before were failed harvests rectified?
This is what his faction means by enterprise:
He can fit all ranks around the table:
Businessmen may hobnob with senators,
While matrons kiss the children of the rest.
Protocol has lapsed with liberality.
What other living god would find the time
To entertain in public or go walkabout
As he has done? We've even seen him dine.
Whether we be palace bred or raised in
Cardboard City, dear, each of us may
Call himself our honoured leader's guest.

Simultaneous with our grateful belches,
Queries as to what we're eating
Mingle with the bookies shouting odds
For those who want a flutter on the show.
Yes, there are female gladiators now
In these emancipated days, amateurish
Maybe; but they can deal each other
Quite a blow with those professional weapons.
What would be the reference now?

Thermodon's daughters they can't be.
These look like girls from the Volga
Beating the shit out of negresses from Fez.
At a stretch, you might say the Amazons
Were fighting a campaign in darkest Africa.
My trivial pursuit has been mythology,
So let me see the line-up on the card.
I'll try to place the dwarfs who come on next,
Slathering for blood in massed battalions.
Frogs and their request might be appropriate
To those pygmies spitted on a trident;
But nature has already bound this lot
In such knotted lumps the retiarius
Will hardly be required to fling his net.

Nor is it time to go home as yet,
Although the shadows lengthen. Next
On the agenda is audience participation:
Easy prizes too, in the shape of maidens
With appropriate zones freshly sewn back on:
Stage-struck celebs who can certainly
Accommodate your ugly line in weaponry
Since they've had experience with asses
And with apes. If they lack such luscious
Virtuosity, you can bet they must have won
Some beauty competition in the provinces.
Here's the Big Knockers corps-de-ballet,
Hotfoot from Lydia, naked to the waist:
They're followed by Iberian flamingos
Bending back until their castanets
Gobble dust behind them; at their rear

The rag, tag and bobtail of theatre:
Robed bone, fire-ship and match-girl
Exchanging puny flares for bits of glass.

But while we go careering after talent,
With a sudden swoop, as from the stars,
Feathered flying objects fall upon us:
Ibises, and partridges, and ostriches.
Well, I've got my hands full of juicy bits
Already, see: I'm not about to let
My bird escape in order to secure
A dinner. Who do you think I am?
Atalanta? I prefer the chase.
But listen to the choric song of pleasure.
Such a circus ought to last forever,
Then nobody would moan about the bread.
Everyone is on their feet, saluting him,
Affectionate, thanking him for now:
But this turns out to be a bloody liberty;
The only freedom Caesar can't allow.

No sooner had the darkness taken over,
Than upwards, from the midst of the arena,
Up through all the gloom and our dyspepsia,
There soared a blazing, spherical, incredible,
Original and splendid ball of fire:
Banishing the horrid powers of darkness,
Weakening the sluggish drug of sleepiness,
So that Hypnos fled to other cities.
Just what happened next, whatever floor-show,
Comic, band or orgy in the afterglow,

Or whether breakfast led to some free lunch
With drinks as ever on the ruling house,
I can't remember. Didn't I pass out,
Or didn't I? For reeling from your Naxian,
I drained myself away into oblivion.

How many years will hand this day of days
To other years for reverent safe-keeping?
Never blot it out at any time, dears.
As long as Saturn hides among the hills
Of Latium, as long as hills are hills;
As long as Father Tiber rolls, and Rome
Remains a cultured city with a Capitol
Beautifully restored to former grandeur
By our present conscientious Emperor,
This memory should flourish as he wills.

[A. H.]

MELIOR'S PLANE-TREE

Where openings gleam and rustles overhang
The liquid shadow on that lake or reservoir
Contrived by Melior, my refined acquaintance,
Stands, or bends, a tree whose dappled trunk
Goes arching from its roots which grip the bank
Towards the water, whence it straightens up,
Stretches aloft, as if it had put down
A surreptitious system through the ripples.
Hardly theme for Phoebus, whose superior
Beams are not accustomed to enquiring here.
Better let the naiads give the game away:
Their song may suit some easy-going faun.

Stampeded herds of nymphs are fleeing Pan
Who seems to want them all, though bent on Pholoe.
She tears on through the brambles, over streams,
Ducks his probing horns, evades the hirsute
Haunches of that billy-goat philanderer.
Across the duelling grove of Janus, past
The filthy den of Cacus, through Quirinal
Fields she bolts, on the balls of frightened feet.
She gains the haven coverts of the Caelian
Only to collapse for want of breath,
And panicked senseless, lies just where today
We lounge within this sanctuary of Melior's.
All she does is huddle, wrapped up tight
Inside her saffron cloak, against the sand

Which skirts the bank. The Goat-God finds her scent
And scampers up – is in the mood to mate –
Pauses to control his jitters, then
Gets over her, suspensefully aflare
Just as the twin horns of the moon appear
Above Diana's brow – she's hunting here,
Having chased a hart raised on the Aventine
Across the seven hills. But seeing Pan
About to mount poor Pholoe, she turns
In fury to attendant whippers-in:
"Damn me, if this vermin doesn't merit
Culling when it decimates our stock!"
She draws a shaft, but simply hasn't time
To string it if her virgin's present zone
Is not to gloss his latest dirty joke,
So flings it in the nymph's direction – not
With customary twang, but feathers first,
Which brush the left hand of the swooning one.
Enough to rouse her. Coming to, she sees
His dangerous condition, its proximity,
And, rather than become some snow-white fodder,
Plunges in, still parcelled in her cloak.

And so she sinks, to cower in the weed
Believing that he'll follow. But he won't.
Baffled into wilting, shaggy-sided,
Not a single scale on him – who never
In his childhood got to learn to swim.
Gruffly and incessantly, the God
Complains that Bromius has it in for him;

That arrow was competing with his prong;
And than a lake there's nothing quite so treacherous.
It's then he sees the plane-tree, which is flexible,
Its trunk a slender stem uplifting countless
Branches, each aspiring to the skies.
This he brings towards him, heaps its crest
With sand which quickly sets, and dips it in
The liquid place which hides his pent desire.
"Grow now as the sign of my intention, tree,
Forever stooping here to mark the secret
Bolt-hole of this less than willing nymph.
Cover up her waters with your foliage;
And, though she well deserves it, don't allow
The sun to dry her out or sting of hail
To lash her flanks: instead bestrew the pool
With scattered leaves – so serve to jolt my memory
As to the mistress of this decent spot
Till riper times, and let all other trees –
Jove's oak, Apollo's bays, the silver poplar
And my pines – prove suitably surprised
By your obedient posture."

                              And the tree,
Trembling with his passion, bent across
The surface, which had risen with her plunge,
And sought for her with loving shadows, hoping for
Her clinging arms – instead the water spurned
Its branches, so it struggled upwards then,
And once again, without a single knot,
The trunk allowed its leaves to seek the sky

As if its roots were bedded in fluidity.
And now that servant of the moon below
Has come to like it, and entices all
Its banished branches back into the pool.

[A. H.]

MELIOR'S PARROT

Popinjay, nonpareil bird, sweet interlocutor,
Ingenious impersonator, dear Parrot, of human speech,
Who has cut off with a brusque doom your conversation?
Only yesterday, poor friend, already fated to die,
You joined us at dinner: till gone midnight we saw you
Hopping from couch to couch, plucking the generous table's
Titbits. You would greet us with well-considered words,
And in due form. But now your lot is the everlasting
Silence of Lethe. Let the popular tale of Phaethon
Give way: it is not only swans who sing their own dirge.
How spacious was your dwelling, how shiny its dome,
Its fence of silver rods with ivory interconnected!
The door that squeaked so shrill at the touch of your beak
Now complains of its own accord; lacking your clamour,
That happy prison, that consecrated fane, gapes empty.

Gather round, you learned birds to whom Nature
Has given the privilege of speech; let Phoebus' raven
Wring his wings, the starling rehearse his sayings by rote,
Along with magpies once the girls who challenged the Muses,
The partridge whose reiterated vocables are slurred and blurred,
And the grieving nightingale taught to speak both Greek and
    Latin:
Groan all at once, conduct your cousin to his burning pyre,
And sing in chorus this dolorous newly-learned lament: –
"The glory and renown of all our airborne orders is dead,
The Parrot, the green and vivid ruler of Orient lands;
Whose aspect neither the jewelled tails of Juno's peacocks,

Nor gamebirds Numidians snare beneath moist southern skies,
Nor pheasants from icy Phasis, are able to outshine.
He had saluted kings and spoken the mighty name
Of Caesar, then set himself to serve a friend aggrieved,
Was next a carefree table-companion, with such address
Could he recite his lines! When he was uncaged, dear Melior,
You were never alone. And he does not go ingloriously
Into the shadows: his ashes fragrant with Assyrian balsam,
His tenuous feathers breathing the scent of Arabian herbs
And Sicanian saffron, spared the weary dullness of age,
He will mount among perfumed flames, a more auspicious
    Phoenix."

[B. S.]

ON A TAME LION KILLED IN THE COLOSSEUM

God knows what it cost you to control
Your temper, make a velvet paw the rule,
Curb your savage instinct and remain
Impervious to the scent of human blood.
How could you walk to heel beside a master
Weaker than you were and agree to come
Bounding at his whistle from your cage
Or at his word return behind its bars?
What did you hope to gain as his retriever,
Relinquishing the duck when he said drop it,
Your jaws relaxed while nuzzling his hand?
Today, for all the odds were on the likelihood
You'd lay the wildest low, you lie here dead:
Not ambushed and surrounded by attackers,
Not hampered by a net or by a snare,
Not launched into a spring against a spear,
Not hoaxed by matted twigs above a pit,
But broken by a creature as it ran from you.
Your cage is free, but you will not return,
While brother lions pace behind locked doors
And shiver at the ignominy done to you.
Their manes droop, they seem ashamed to look,
As hooks are fixed to tow away your corpse;
And now their foreheads wrinkle into frowns.

That blow which brought about this sorry state
Did not entirely blot you out immediately:

Your courage seemed to kindle at your fall
And hauled your spirit back to loose a roar
And gnash your grinders; menacing in death
As you had never been from day to day.
You seemed a soldier, knowing he was done for,
Though struggling to block the hostile's path
With hand upraised despite a failing blade.
Leonine, you tottered, robbed of pride,
Yet forcing further roars and harder eyes
While gasping for your prey as for your breath.
And though a moment later you fell down,
A rich reward goes with you from the ring:
As if you were some gladiator then,
The star of several seasons, now a carcass
Measuring your length in sprinkled sand,
The mob groaned, the Senate heaved a sigh,
And it was sad to see you pulled away.
And when you think of tigers we have seen
From Scythia, and Libyan panthers too,
Bears from beyond the Rhine and aurochs herds
From Egypt whose demise is no to-do,
Consider, lion, what effect you had
Upon our Ruler, who has seen it all.
You moved him: I saw moisture in his eyes.

[A. H.]

TO HIS WIFE

Haven't we held our waking lives
        in common always, and our nights?
Yet I cannot share this depression of yours,
        cannot imagine why you sigh
So anxiously. Why don't you sleep?
        It can't be an indiscretion. I've no fear
Of that, nor of some rival passion.
        The very idea is a joke in the meanest taste.

Yours is not the breast for poisoned darts.
        A frowning Nemesis
Must keep to her Rhamnusian plinth,
        even if her stone ears catch my words.
Even were I uprooted, sent abroad,
        and set two long decades of siege and seafaring,
You would be here, untainted,
        refusing a thousand suitors, doing nothing

So coquettish as to unweave some vaunted web
        – but simply being straightforward,
Promptly showing all the door,
        and resolutely locking up. So why
The furrowed forehead, the turbulence
        that overwhelms your countenance?
Can't you accept that I need to prepare
        my retirement, being distinctly

The worse for wear, planning to go home
　　　　to my Campania, my *heimat* there,
Returning these limbs to the loam
　　　　from which they sprung, as it were?
What is so bad about that, for heaven's sake?
　　　　You were never really game
For gadding about or circuses
　　　　– you always said you found sport unattractive –

Nor have you ever been terribly keen
　　　　on the theatre. No, my dear,
You were seldom for crowds, more for
　　　　sheltered atrium, culture without gaudiness.
It's not as if I were planning to take you
　　　　on some sublime, storm-driven trip.
Although, if I were, what of it?
　　　　Say I intended to explore the Arctic

Or to cast off for some ultimate Thule
　　　　or seek the sevenfold sources of the Nile,
Normally you'd be the one to insist
　　　　I stop procrastinating – you after all,
Whom Venus so kindly united with
　　　　my initial flush, my life's insurance, you
Who I got stuck on as a virgin,
　　　　you who fixed my inexperienced dithering –

You it is whose rein I nod to in my steady gait,
      answering to the bit since broken-in:
Well and truly wedded to the bridle.
      When I won the golden wreath at Alba
You were who most made me feel
      transfigured with your tight embrace.
Remember how your showered my bays
      with kisses? When the Capitol

Chose to reject my strains you were as
      disconsolate as I was. How you railed,
At the sheer forgetfulness of Jupiter,
      the clique that runs the poetry establishment.
Haven't *I* kept you awake before:
      preliminary attempts at lines and whole nights
Of murmured sound? – you who alone
      shared the secret of the pains I took

To bring my epic up: our years together
      constitute my *Thebaid*.
And when I was very nearly snatched
      into the shadows recently, already in my ears
The cold babble of Lethe, yours
      were the sad eyes that kept me seeing.
Pitying you, Lachesis surely
      knotted some extension to my thread,

And certainly the high gods feared
       the stamina of your sustained reproaches.
Why, after that, do you hesitate to go with me
       on this, this insignificant journey
To such a desirable bay? Ah, well,
       it seems at last to have worn away – that loyalty
That was a byword, that had more than
       proved its worth, that made you one

With the daughters of an old-time Rome,
       with models like Penelope.
Had not wise Ulysses put his foot down,
       how she would have loved to sail for Troy!
Nothing deters true lovers, you see.
       This one frets and that one frowns.
Laodamia's made a Maenad by departure.
       And you can hold your own with such

As these for laying down your life
       and taking mine up. Is it not your nature?
Do you not *still* burn more than
       a single taper to your former husband,
Loitering over his ashes, editing his relics
       while quoting him with a practically
Inappropriate vehemence, even
       though you've espoused another's cause?

Is not your care as zealous for your daughter?
          Are you not as conscientious
As a mother, if not more? And don't you
          have her in mind now most of the time?
The darker the night, the deeper your projects
          concern her. No seabird floats
On a love more serene, no songbird sings
          to her young in spring more sweetly.

She is the problem, though, isn't she? Isn't she?
          Obviously her business holds you up:
A bird in the hand, but unmated as yet,
          wasting youth and beauty in some fruitless
Passing of each day. But still,
          her day will come, with its consuming torches,
As she deserves, given such a pleasant
          manner, such a fetching outward glance,

Whether refusing to hang up her lute
          or tuning the voice her father adored to my airs,
Teaching the muses a thing or two,
          or flinging about her snow-white arms.
The fact is, her brand of modest innocence
          far exceeds her artistic applications.
We can only hope the wiles of love
          prove a touch more nimble than her talents.

Clearly it would shame the Cytherean
        to witness such a sprite remain a spinster.
However, Rome is not the sole
        cornucopia of ripe and ready bachelors
Or festal flames – my country harbours
        sons-in-law as well, you know.
And though the baleful crater of Vesuvius
        may have spewed erratic storms of flame,

It hasn't as yet been entirely successful
        in its plan to drain our panicked cities
Of their males: a residue remains,
        a residue of lads in fact – which flourishes
Among the western porticos and tall facades
        that send their valediction to each sunset.
There's a port that welcomes all the world,
        Begirt with walls to rival the stupendous

Scale of Rome, its towers manned by immigrants,
        Trojan ones. Its backdrop is my stamping ground,
My little city, filled to bursting,
        yet with queues at every gate; a city named
Parthenope, who traced Dione's cooing call
        to fertile land as promised by Apollo.
This is home, not thorny Thrace,
        nor lion-haunted Libya after all.

Into some nice garden here, I'm eager to
        transplant you and install you in
A climate of mild winters and cool summers
        by a shore where breezes hardly
Lift the fringes of our harmless sea,
        where peace rules unusurped by harsh disturbance,
And life is quite sedately paced
        while sleep maintains a night-long continuity.

No madness in our courts, my love,
        no laws unsheathed in cutting litigation since
Our statutes come from the heart.
        Natural justice needs no rods or axes.
Do I need to emphasize the vistas and
        embellishments of a region hardly bettered
By some painter of imaginary scenes?
        Temples, halls, and columns, many columns.

The theatres, one covered, one exposed.
        The celebrated contests, the quinquennials,
Which rather take the lustre off the Capitol.
        No need to mention the curve of the bay
Or prate about the "freedom of Menander".
        Country folk allow a self-fulfilment:
Roman strictures laced with Grecian tolerance.
        You will find a cultivated hinterland

Provides you with a steaming spa at Baiae,
        mythic reference at the Sibyl's cave,
Marvellous views from the cape with its Trojan oar.
        Then Gaurus has consecrated wineries
Where the stock flows over every
        Bacchus-prompted spur. And of course we're
Hardly far from Capri, where the steady
        Pharus holds a beacon to an errant moon,

Much to the delight of frightened sailors.
        We can call on Pollius, my celebrated friend.
Speckled panthers lope along his terraces,
        high up on the Surrentine escarpment.
We can take the mud-baths, visit the rebuilding
        since the lava-flow, or what you will.
Must I keep reiterating benefits?
        No, because you know your proper role.

Enough for me to say, "This land produced me.
        Its plenty made us one an age ago.
Take it on trust that this mother of mine
        can be counted on now to adopt you as well."
I'll not let my tongue run away with me
        nor be so churlish as to doubt your loyalty.
You will go with me, if not before me,
        rather than remain behind in Rome, my dear,

Only to find nothing in the Quirinal arcade
        or wander at a loss along the Tiber.

    [A. H.]

THANKSGIVING TO THE EMPEROR
AUGUSTUS GERMANICUS DOMITIANUS

Virgil, who brought great Aeneas to Laurentian lands,
Praises the royal banquets of Sidonian Elissa;
And Homer, who completes Ulysses' drawn-out seafaring,
Paints in enduring verse the feasting of Alcinous:
But I, on whom Caesar has now for the first time bestowed
The joy of a sacred dinner, to mount to my Prince's table,
How can my lyre make known my devotion, discharge
My gratitude? Not even if Smyrna and Mantua bound
My head with their fragrant laurels, could I utter
Adequate words. I seem to recline amidst the stars
With Jove and to take from Ganymede's outstretched hand
Immortal wine! I have let barren years go by,
And this is my earliest day, the threshold of life.
Is it You, the Ruler of Nations, the Great Father
Of the subject world, You Hope of Mankind, You Care of Gods,
Whom I behold? Is it then given to look on Your face
Amidst wine and food and right not to rise to my feet?

Domitian's dwelling, vast, famed not for a hundred pillars,
But as many as could support, were Atlas pardoned,
The skies and the gods! Jupiter's neighbouring palace
Is stunned, the Powers rejoice that You inhabit
As fine a seat. No hurry to ascend to the mighty skies:
The fabric spreads so wide; the extensive concourse's sweep,
More open than a plain, encloses massive volumes
Of air, is less than its Master only: He fills the house,

His mighty energy makes it rejoice. And here contend
Libyan mountain, and shining Ilian, and abundance
Of Chian and Syenite marbles, and that which competes
With sea-green Doris, and Lunan enough to carry the
    columns.
Far upward yet the view: one's weary eyesight grasps
The roof and one deems it the golden ceiling of heaven.
Here, when Caesar has ordered it, Roman chiefs
And knightly bands at a thousand tables recline together:
Ceres, her robe girded up, and Bacchus work hard
To supply them. So bounteously spun the wheels of divine
Triptolemus; so Bacchus shaded the naked hills,
And sober farmlands, beneath the shoots of his vines.

I had no leisure for food, the Moorish oaken board
Supported on ivory columns, the troops of girls in waiting,
So great was my desire to gaze at Him, at Him,
His tranquil countenance, His majesty serene
That tempered its rays, with modesty furling the flags
Of His estate. The grace He veiled shone nevertheless
In His visage, and even thus outlandish tribes
Of barbarian enemies would have known Him had they seen.
Just so does Mars recline in Rhodope's cool vale,
His horse unyoked; and so does Pollux, relaxed
After Spartan wrestling, dispose his well-oiled limbs;
So lies Bacchus by Ganges, while the Indians howl;
So mighty Hercules, returning after his awesome tasks,
Was pleased to lay his side on his lion-skin blanket.
Domitian, I speak of trifles, nothing to equal Your visage:
Such is heaven's king when he revisits Aethiopia's coasts

And Ocean's bound and, features suffused with holy nectar,
Commands the Muses to sing their mystical hymns
And Apollo to celebrate the triumph at Phlegra.

May the gods grant (they are said often to attend to us
Mortal souls) that You shall surpass, twice and thrice over,
Your father's age! May You send Your appointed gods to heaven,
Dedicate temples, and dwell in Rome! Often may You
Fling wide the gates of the year, greeting Janus with new lictors,
Often renew the Capitol's garlanded competition!
The day when You vouchsafed to me the sacred blessings
Of Your festal board, after long interval came at last
Like that when, beneath the hills of Trojan Alba, I sang
Now German battle array, now Dacian fights,
And on me Your hand placed Pallas' golden wreath.

[B. S.]

THE FEAST AT THE LORD GOD'S

The Royal feast of Sidonian Dido is sung
By him who brought great Aeneas
By the meadows of the Laurentine,
The banquet of Alcinous is recalled
In deathless verse by him who told the return
Over the seas of Ulysses, the wind-weathered one,
But I – to whom Caesar has only just now,
For the first time ever, afforded the right
To partake of the *bliss* of his holy banquet
In my own lifetime, and rise still alive,
From an Emperor's table – how shall I sing
My resounding thanks, for the supper, I mean,
How tune my lyre to the theme of it? Nay,
Though my brow be bound and blessed
With the fragrant bays of Smyrna and of Mantua,
Not even so shall my strains be enough.
I seem to be feasting right in the heart of
Heaven with Jove. From the Trojan's hand,
And not in mime, I receive immortal wine.
Eternal time! How barren now the years
Before this! Here am I announced! My days begin.
This is the threshold of my life.
Ruler of the conquered planet, Father,
Hope of mankind, love-object
Of the gods, dost thou appear to me
As I recline here? Is is really thou?
And dost thou suffer me to see thy face,
Thy face, which is actually there, above the flagon?

Surely, I must rise to make this toast,
And not to omit them, start with things remote:
The hall itself, it's plenteous, as to columns,
Not merely graced with a hundred or so,
But with the multitude required
To lift the gods were Atlas given notice.
Neighbouring vibrations from the Thunderer
Testify that he finds thine sublime. Thy temple.
All of the gods rejoice that thine's a home
As fair as theirs. Thou hast no need to join them,
So spacious is the pile! Its hall a plain
But more so, closing in a swathe
Of sky within its sweep, and unsurpassed
Save by its Lord. His presence fills the space,
Gives it its soul, and *how* that delights it.
Rivalry perhaps reflects his beams
From Libyan marble, paired to that of Ilium;
While resting upon Syenite are Chian
Slabs and weighty blocks of sea-grey stone.
All this supported by moonlight merely it seems!
So high the roof above, we'll term it vault.
The weary eye can scarcely to its zenith.
Call it not ridge! The ceiling being that
Of the very golden heavens, you might think;
Such being the edifice where he commanded
Romulus' stock and the knights in array
To take their places at the thousand tables,
There, with tucked up hem, in person, Ceres
Toiled with Bacchus, willingly in service.
There sat they together, knights and nobles,
As amid such plenty onetime rolled

The wheels of heaven-born Triptolemus;
As did wild Lyaeus in his heyday
Bounteously overshadow scenes
Barren and tilled with his o'erladen vines.

But not upon the feast, nor on each lovely
Couch of Moorish citron set on mini-pillars
Delicately carved from precious tusks,
Nor on the panorama of his family –
On him, on him alone, I could but gaze.
My eyes beheld serenity of countenance:
While tempered brightness with a tranquil majesty
Gently abated the well-proclaimed pomp
Of his grandeur; though what he would hide,
That *radiance*, shone out upon his brow.
Even the Serbian foe, the Iraqi, even the Martian
Who knew him not, would know him,
Know his Mekon, surely, by such splendour.
Thus calmly after stabling his steeds
Gradivus rests in Rhodope's chill valleys;
So Pollux lounging from the lists at Therapne
Lays down his glistering limbs; So Euhan
Lofted on the wailing banks of Ganges
'Mid the abandoned *jouissance* of his Indians;
So grim Alcides, trailing inert bystanders,
Returns to rest his bulk upon the lion skin . . .

[A. H.]

What clangour is this, of obdurate flint
Battered by the hammer that rings out
Mightily against the stone-clad Appian
On the side of it nearest the sea?
It can't be Libyans – doing another stint –
Nor any belligerent foreign chap
Steering illegal squads across Campania,
Nor yet a Nero, slicing escarpments
And channelling sludge through each gap.
But he, who, with courts of law,
Blocks retrospective vendettas;
He, who restores the green-belt to Ceres,
Weeding out vines and re-affirming
Sober agrarian policy, he who censors
Any snip that seeks to freeze good looks
And renovates the fired pile of the Thunderer,
He who puts Peace back in place
And inspects Heaven's street-lights, thus
Establishing a decent *Flavian* Presidency
Up there in the night-sky. He it is,
Well-wearied of the gross impunctuality
Brought about by saturated plains,
Who cuts through this knot of directions
And obviates the affliction of
The detour that dogged us of old.
Stability's his middle name,
Who's laid a firm foundation down,
To beat the tacky sand here,

Pleased to bring the Sibyl's cave, and all
The coastal landmarks, spas and dells
A sight closer to the seven hills.

Here, at a snail's pace, before, the traveller
Borne by a single axle, teetered
On the yawing tree, while his wheels got eaten
By the vicious mud beneath him.
Half-way across this plain was worse
Than the shudder-inducing curse of a voyage
By sea. Nothing got you there faster:
Gunge in the grooves retarded your hoof-clogged
Animal, that could hardly even plod
Along the water-logged joke of a course
And whinnied continually under its burden,
Not to mention its heavily ballasted yoke.
Now an entire day's journey takes an hour
Or two at the most. No swifter fare ye
Through the heavens, ye birds,
Nor swifter wing, with overt sail, ye boats!

First, the job was to incise the furrows,
Demarcate the shoulder of the road
And scoop the earth out to the depth demanded,
Next to fill the trench with compact stuff,
Lay the groundwork for the convex camber
Of the ridge above – and guarantee
A base that should stay tremor-free, and not
Afford a merely treacherous bed
For slabs ordained to bear an imperium's load;
Then use blocks to bind the jigsaw in,

Ram it in from the sides with well-braced wedges.
Work for teeming gangs! Some fell the forest,
Leaving mountains naked, some shave down
Required stakes and beams with rasps,
Some assemble the pavers, bonding these
With baked clay and dingy bits of pumice.
Others drain up-welling pools by hand
Or seek distractions for encroaching tributaries.
Crews like these could put a hole through Athos,
Bridge the Hellespont without pontoons
And mix seas by severing some Isthmus.

Shorelines seek adjustment, woods
Are on the move, while uproar ricochets
Off embattled walls along the way.
Echoes bounce drunkenly back and forth
Or spill down hillsides. Meditation's
Shattered at the oracle, and wrinkles
Sour idyllic ponds as industry
Goads on sluggish backwaters remorselessly.

But now Vulturnus lifts his yellow
Features and bedraggled locks
Plastered with water-weed; surfacing
To lean against the big arch of
The new-built Caesar bridge and spout
In a gravelly voice these words:
"Generous fixer of my fields,
Who, while I poured o'er trackless vales
In ignorance of how to flow within
Agreed controls called *banks*, didst choose

To bind me to the contract of a strict
Sense of channel, look at me!
A onetime delinquent, dangerous, who
One wouldn't push one's skiff into,
Don't I put up with a bridge now?
Am I not trodden on with impunity?
Pooh! I, who was once just a flood, you see,
– Shame on me, shame on me! –
You have caused to embark on the career
Of being a river, thank you very much!
As such, my obedience is worthwhile
Because I have conceded to your rule,
And you will be the one in perpetuity
Renowned as the enforcer of my destiny.
I really do appreciate the embankments,
And the way your dredgers do not permit me
To foul myself anymore, and how
You've siphoned off the obnoxious stain
Of my common dirt so that I never
Soil the Tyrrhenian deep with muddy feet,
Unlike the Bagrada, that baggage of a river,
Polluting Punic fields in a *Cinyphian* manner.
Now I can saunter sparkling into the sea
And gurgitate with my neighbours unashamedly."

As he intones, some finishing touches
Are added to the bridge, a marble stretch,
Raised to a truly awe-inspiring apex:
Its portal made immortal surely by
A perfect rainbow of a regal gate-way
Hung with our Führer's Ligurian gems

And bellicose trophies. This is where
The step quickens as it takes the turn,
Leaving the Appian Way to groan.
Now we can really get going, everything
Doing the pulling delights in the pace,
As when the sails catch the breeze at last
And rowers feel a sense of added impetus.
Bid farewell to the Tiber at dawn,
And you can be scooping out Lucrine shells
By the seaside before twilight.
Nothing impedes the impatient, these days.
Approach, then, ye mysterious Orientals,
Very deservedly fallen under the sway
Of our triumphal father in Rome,
This is the cut-price luxury route.
Waft here the faster, ye laurels!

That said, what is this apparition,
White of hair and bleached of hood,
Who stands now at the vanishing point
Of this new highway leading straight
To where Apollo indicates her sanctum
With a temple? Should I doubt
The wavering sight before my eyes,
Or is it the Sibyl herself with the bays
I've just invoked? 'Tis she. She bears them
Out of her cave. So let my secular
Lyre retire, since a sacred chord
Is about to be struck. Oh, me, shut up!
Her head rolls this way and that.
She roams in a highly excited state

All over the free-way, then, at last,
Opens an ancient yet maidenly mouth:

"Did I not ask both river and field to be patient?
One will come, one will, one will,
Blessed on High, to lift everything up –
Rank and rotting woodland, coast
Crawling with mosquitoes – using
Phenomenal bridges, causeways. Ai!
A God is he, sent earthwards for our good
By Jupiter, to be his steward here.
None worthier than he has held the reins
Since under my guidance Aeneas
Eager to eat of his future, went below,
Into the prescient groves of dark Avernus,
Boldly to come up again and go
About his business. Friend is he to Peace,
By being terrible in will to harm,
More bountiful than any bush in nature,
More powerful, a better son than Phaeton
To his father, for were *he* to drive
The flaming fiery chariot, you, India,
Would be all moisture wreathed in cloud,
While Libya would be florider than Florida,
And bathers could enjoy the melted snowcaps.

Hail, then, leader of men, progenitor
Of deities! Whose godhead I foresaw
And appropriately acknowledged.
Now you need no longer pore
Over my words as unrolled on rotting papyrus,

Deciphering the liturgical lore
Of the fifteen priests, but, meriting this,
Hear me speak my prophecy in person.
I have seen what chain of years
The shining sisters weave for you,
Centuries on centuries attend,
Outlasting sons and sons of sons,
A tranquil age of eternal youth is yours:
A trove of years like Nestor's, as they say,
Added to those notched up by Tithonus,
Plus the fistful I squeezed out of Apollo.

Already the North snows allegiance,
Soon the East will afford you triumphs.
Go, where Hercules' wanderlust led
And Bacchus's roaming took him.
Travel beyond the burning sun, the stars,
The Nile's wellhead and the snows of Atlas.
Blessed with every honorific increment,
Either mount or choose, as you wish, to refuse
The unassailable chariots of your wrath.
So long as the plutonium blasts, and the fly-pasts
Thunder over resurrected towers,
Indomitable, extend your sway,
And live you as long as this road shall last,
Outdistancing the Appian's ancient Way."

[A. H.]

ODE TO SEPTIMIUS SEVERUS

Charmed with my rural smallholding
Where Alba tends her Trojan hearths,
I salute with this exotic lyre
Brave and eloquent Severus.

Immolated by high-risen suns
Winter retreats to arctic Parrhasus,
Sea and land beam in sunshine,
Aquilo fragments in Zephyrs.

Each tree is now coiffed with vernal
Foliage whence sound the fresh laments
And under-rehearsed lyric odes
Composed by the birds in silent winter.

My little land, my ever-watchful
Hearth and rooftree sooty from much
Domestic smoke, and Bacchus decanted
From the jar he fermented in, console me.

No woolly thousands bleat,
No cow moos for her paramour,
The mute fields resound only
When their master is moved to sing.

Yet after my fatherland these lands
Are dearest to me; here Pallas,
And Caesar, crowned my songs
With the golden olive wreath,

When you wholeheartedly
Rooted for your friend in sweet peril –
As Castor trembled at the commotion
When Pollux fought Amycus.

Did Leptis merged in the remote Syrtes
Bear you? – then she shall bear Indian
Harvests and plunder the precious
Cinnamon of the perfumed Sabaeans.

Who would think Septimius had not
Crawled on every hill in Rome
Or deny that, weaned, he had quenched
His thirst at Juturna's fountain?

Likewise your manhood: African shallows
Left unexplored, you straightway entered
Ausonian havens; an adoptive son,
You sailed upon Tuscan deeps.

A child among senators' sons you grew up
Content with the dress of your modest rank
Yet seeking, with innate nobility,
Immeasurable achievements.

You have no Punic dress-sense or accent,
No incomer's mind: Italian, Italian!
(Among our Roman knights are some
Who would find their level in Libya . . .)

Delightful your voice in the muttering
Law-courts, never venal your eloquence;
Quietly peaceful your sword in its sheath,
Drawn only at your friends' behest.

More often, however, your heart seeks
Rural quiet, now in your father's house
In Veientine country, now in historic
Cures, and now in lofty Hernica.

Here you will put forth more things
In freely pacing measures and diction,
But mindful at times of me resume
The lyre laid by in a modest grotto.

    [B. S.]

VINDEX

One evening, as I sauntered down the Mall,
A truant from my epic, since my hankering
Was not for metre, I ran into Vindex
Who kindly bore me off with him to dine.
I confess I still hang out a candle
Commemorating that nocturnal spell:
It wasn't merely casual degustation
Or feast esteemed for where its dishes hail from
By those who toast the furthest flung surprise
In vintages pre-dating public files.
Our invites prove a burden when gourmets
Insist upon us knowing grouse from crane;
Whether goose's *mons Veneris* is
A choicer offering than gander's priapus;
Why the Umbrian boar is mainly brawn
Compared to the refinement of the Tuscan;
And just upon which mythic littoral
The bower be of the best oyster of all.

Our fodder, though, was rather more *nouvelle*.
We munched upon the salad of the intellect,
Our chit-chat enlivened by the Hippocrene.
We cracked a dozen jokes at every lamp
Refilled to see us through the deep mid-winter,
And kept the sleep away, till Castor's twin
Came tutting at us from the land of Nod,
And through the gauzes then the dawn came in,
Mocking at the remnants of our Marathon.

But wasn't that a night? It should have been
Two nights rolled into one, with mated moons;
As once in Tiryns Hermes stalled the light.
Only deep sea divers should aspire
To raid the pearl-filled oyster of its date.
Oh sweet night so delicate and rare,
Where there was anything but meagre fare
So far as intellectual matters went,
Your faint ghost does well to linger here.

Never in my life have I set eyes
On such a host of pre-Augustan artefacts:
Ivories and bronzes, and some pieces done
So perfectly in wax they seemed about
To burst into some comment on our badinage.
For no one has a better eye than Vindex.
He can put a price on any object
You give into his hands, and he can date it
To the Kalend, cite its forge or quarry.
Vindex can confirm that your discobolus
Was one which cost the knowing Myron sleep,
And warn you if it's likely your Praxiteles
Was conjured into being by a chiseller.
He can say which ivory was polished
By the living finger of the Pisan school;
Which torso is the work of Polyclitus,
What line in silhouette betrays an Apelles.
Vindex likes to ponder his collection
When he isn't stroking his guitar:
This is the obsession that compels him
To cancel his engagements at the venue.

Among his artworks, guardian and god
Of unencumbered table, lounged a Hercules
I coveted so much I could have eaten it:
And even as I delved into the salad-bowl
I banqueted my eyes upon this masterpiece.
Such majesty informed its cast, such power
Put within its mass, you'd say the deity,
Yes, the breathing deity resided there;
And he has agreed to pose for Lysippus!
A striking superhuman to his mind,
If practically no better than a midget,
Since he rises but a foot above his base.
We look him up and down, though, and declare
That here we have that strangler of the brute
That rampaged in Nemea; here the thews
Which brought the old shillelagh into play
And smashed the Argo's paddles into kindling.
Bulk is not what does it, what displays
This famous set of pectorals is pretty small:
It took the very devil of a skill
To bring it off, and in the artist's palm
Uncommon strength to dream up a Colossus,
Where we might see a mascot on its place-mat.
It couldn't have been wrought by any primitive
Hobgoblin in the caves of Ida: this
Has far too much fine detail. It's so minuscule,
It would have given Cyclops quite a squint
To labour at it. As for Philoctetes,
He hasn't time to go about a likeness
Of his master, since he sailed from Lemnos
To burnish up the armour of the Pantheon.

You shouldn't think this figure too uncouth
To play the majordomo to these gatherings
Of connoisseurs relaxed without emetics:
This Hercules instructed poor Molorchus
On how to dress a truly sumptuous sacrifice,
And when lit-up, suggested that a priestess
Should join him on a couch reserved for Goddesses.
Rising from the cinders of his funeral,
He downs the nectar Juno has prohibited,
And jovially insists that we carouse with him.
His brother's cup is dandled by a hand;
The other grips his club for some support.
His lion's pelt is thrown across a rock
As if he said, "How nice to find a seat!"

Inspired work, and yet, you know, its merit
Is somewhat overshadowed by its provenance:
Alexander probably commissioned it
For the *genius loci* of his table-cloth
Wherever it was spread when on campaign.
The very hand that tore the crowns off kings
Or fitted them, that ordered cities razed,
Would scratch his metal belly with a fingernail.
Tomorrow's fight would occupy the cutlery,
And Hercules would stand in for his master,
Who'd kiss him for heroics in the field.
Inevitably later he would be informed
Of just exactly how the day was carried;
How India was drunk on Alexander,
Not subjugated to the sway of Bromius,
Whose manacles were more the stuff of legend;

How his ram had battered mighty Babylon,
How he had undone the Pelasgians
And brought Peloponnesus to its knees.
And Hercules would tell us if he could
That of the cities brought beneath his yoke
He only made apologies for Thebes.
And when it all went sour in the end,
The thread of his achievement having shrivelled,
Alexander sipped the lethal draught
With toasts to absent friends he'd given poison,
And shuddered when he saw the figurine
Break into sweat – or was it condensation?

What with so much melted down since then,
A Lysippus is something of a rarity:
But Hercules got lucky and turned up again
Among the semi-civilized in Africa.
Hasdrubal had had him off of Hamilcar,
But Hannibal pumped iron like an Atlas
And had him off his brother, fist to fist.
Hannibal would send up his libations
By sinking his brass-hat in troughs of blood
Let by his double-blade and giving Hercules
A drenching that was loathsome to the god
Of combat, who abhorred a foreigner
So steeped in Latin gore, so very keen
To set alight the towered town of Romulus.
Hated him, yes, even when he dedicated
Women, wine, and beef to his authority
While spinning out that holiday in Capua
Which cost him all he'd ever won by massacre:

For Mars had not forgiven him the fire
That gutted his arena at Saguntus:
A living town transformed into a pyre
As an excuse to drag us into war with him.

When Hannibal was all washed up, the bronze
Fell into more discriminating hands.
Accustomed as it was to stately homes,
And chary of its purchaser's credentials,
The trophy now adorned the feasts of Sulla,
Who was gratified to hear his name enhanced
Its run of owners; fond of all proscriptions,
Approving of its pedigree of masters,
Although perhaps the first of them to pass
Contentedly away amid the fruits
Of labours which made Hercules redundant.

Today, I can assure you, noble masterpiece,
That being an immortal not a statue,
You'll never cast aspersions on the value
Of your present owner: not a king,
Rather a disciple of antiquity,
Generally acknowledged to be upright,
And willing to illuminate the visitor
Come to take a stroll about his sculpture-court.
Vestinus was his mentor, who in youth
Could outbid his elders in the auction-rooms.
Vindex has inherited the mantle.

Here, then, be seated on your pelt
To listen to the plectrum as it strikes

Against the strings, and not the clash of arms.
A bronze, lyre and bay-leaf composition:
This is what must serve to whet the appetite
In the Spartan dining-room of Vindex
Who only recently released a ballad
All about the hell you raised in Ilium,
In Trilium and Thrace and snowy Stymphalos.
How you rustled cattle for a living once,
Reputedly a vandal and a hooligan
Who desecrated temples, burgled galleries,
Penetrated catacombs and mortuaries
To rob the dead of monumental masonry,
Stripped the choicest ornaments off girls
And generally gave everyone the jitters.
Neither that expansive man of Macedon,
Nor Hannibal the horrid, nor the bluff,
Uncompromising Sulla could have sung of you
In such a lovely voice, with so much soul.
Lysippus, who got you into shape,
Sleeps at peace now, knowing you reside
With Vindex – better for it, on the whole.

[A. H.]

JOCULAR LINES TO PLOTIUS GRYPUS

Yes, it is *very* droll, Grypus,
That you send me a book for a book ...
But even that may seem urbane
If now you send me something worthwhile:
To persevere in such a joke, Grypus, would be
Beyond a joke.
              Look, let's balance the books.
Mine was wrapped in red, new paper,
A beautiful knob each end, it cost me
Trouble plus half a crown. But yours –
Worm-eaten, rotting with mould,
Like a book soaked in cheap olive oil,
Or wrapping Nile incense, or pepper,
Or smelling of Byzantine fish –
Not even containing the speeches
You thundered when young to all three forums
Or the hundred judges (before Domitian
Gave you control of the corn supply,
Put you in charge of all roads' staging-posts) –
But, out of some wretched book-peddler's box,
Old Marcus Brutus's mouthings, price
More or less one dud Caligula sixpence –
That's your gift.
             Was there a shortage
Of rag caps cobbled together
From worn-out cloaks, or scraps of papyrus,
Or Carian figs, or Theban dates,
Nowhere a squash of plums or tiny figs

Packed in disposable wrappers,
No dried-out wicks, or thrown-away
Onions' jackets, and not so much as an egg,
No fine grits and no coarse grain,
Nowhere the slimy house of an arching snail
Who wandered afar on Cinyphian plains,
No rancid bacon-fat or tasteless ham,
Lucanian sausage or leaden haggis,
No salt, or butter, or cheese,
Or cakes of green saltpetre,
Moscato wine (boiled, grapes and all),
Or must muddied with sugary lees –
How *could* you not give me smelly tapers,
Or a little knife, or a tiny notebook,
Or bottled grapes, or cheap crocks
Thrown on some wheel at Cumae –
Why not a complete set – don't jump! –
Of plain white cups and pots?

                                        Yet indeed,
A fair dealer, your scales correct,
You weigh my measure precisely.
But if, half-dead, I get up
And bring you my morning greetings,
Must *you* greet *me* at *my* house?
Or you've cheered me up with an excellent dinner –
Do *I* owe *you* a similar feast?

I'm angry with you, Grypus. Still, fare *well* –
Only don't, with your usual pleasantry,
Promptly send back jocular lines.

    [B. S.]

IN MEMORY OF MY FATHER

Father, grant me yourself from Elysian springs
A dour command of grieving song, the beat
Of an ominous lyre. It is not permitted to stir
The Delian caves or initiate Cirrha's accustomed work
Without you. Whatever Apollo lately ordained
In Corycian shade, or Bacchus upon Ismarian hills,
I have unlearned. Parnassus' woollen band has fled
My hair. I have been aghast at defunctive yew
Stealing among the ivy, the bays – unnatural! – parching.
Yet I, inspired, had set myself to extol the deeds
Of great-hearted kings, to equal in singing lofty Mars.
Who makes my barren heart decay? And who, the Apollo
In me quenched, has drawn cold clouds before my mind?
The goddesses stand dismayed about the seer, and sound
No pleasant music with fingers or voice. Their leader leans
Her head on her silent lyre, as after the rape of Orpheus
She stood by Hebrus and gazed at the herds now deaf,
And groves immobile, since that song was taken away.

But you, whether, let go from the flesh, you reach
Up the steeps, review the shining tracts and bases of nature,
And find what is God, whence fire, what pathway leads
The sun, what lessens the moon, and what the cause that can
Restore her when waned, and you extend the bounds
Of famed Aratus; or whether, in Lethe's sequestered pastures,
By conclave of heroes and blessed spirits, you, yourself
No duller shade, attend upon ancient Homer and Hesiod,
Make music in turn and mix your song with theirs:

Supply a voice and talent, father, to my large grief.
For having thrice traversed the sky and thrice annulled
Her features, the moon has seen my sluggish, woeful vigils
Unsolaced by Art: for since your pyre incarnadined
My face, and I gathered your ashes with streaming eyes,
My lowly craft is disesteemed. At first I hardly free
My mind for these things, and essay with drooping hands,
With flowing eyes, to rid my lassitude of silent care,
That leans upon the tomb in which you rest
And possess our acres, where after Aeneas' death
Starry Ascanius builded Alba upon the Latian hills,
Since he contemned the plains bedaubed with Phrygian blood,
His mischief-omened stepmother's regal dowry.
Here I lament you – the breath of Sicanian crocuses
Does not exhale more gently, nor rare cinnamon gathered
By rich Sabaeans, nor Arabia's fragrant harvest –
I lament in Pierian song; you deserve full measure
Of holy offerings: O accept the groans and pain
Of a son, and tears few fathers have ever received.

I wish it were my lot to tender an altar to your shade,
A work matching temples – to raise an airy fabric
Higher than Cyclopes' crags, or pyramids' daring masonry,
And to border your mound with a large grove!
There I had surpassed the tribute of Anchises' tomb,
The Nemean grove, and the games for crippled Pelops.
There no band of many Greeks would cleave the air
With Oebalus' discus, no sweat of horses would water
The ground, or the eroded track resound with hoof-beats:
Only Apollo's choir would be there; I would duly

Praise you, father, and bind on you the poet's leafy prize.
I myself, as priest of the shades and of your soul,
With wet eyes would lead a dirge, from which neither Cerberus
With all his mouths nor Orpheus' spells could turn you away.
And there, as I sang your character and deeds, perhaps
You had not rated mine lower than Homer's mighty speech,
And your fatherly kindness had even held me Virgil's equal.

Why does the mother who sits bereft by her son's still-tepid
    mound
Assail more than I the gods, and the Sisters' brazen threads –
And why does she who observes her youthful husband's pyre
And wins through obstructing hands and the grabbing crowd,
With her blazing husband to die, if it be permitted?
Greater even than theirs, perhaps, does my reproach
Strike Tartarus and the gods: these obsequies even foreign eyes
May pity. Yes, not only Nature and Fatherhood
Have lent themselves to the grieving rite: you were snatched
From me at the threshold of your Fate, father, and underwent
Hard Tartarus in your prime. For Grecian Erigone
Did not bewail more scantly Icarius obliterated
By savage rustics' crime, than Andromache her son Astyanax
Dropped from the Phrygian tower. Indeed, Erigone stifled
Her sighs in a noose, but the other sank to serving,
After great Hector's funeral rites, a Thessalian husband.

I shall not bring to my father's pyre as tribute
The funeral music the swan transmits when sure of his doom:
Nor that with which the winged Tyrrhenian Sirens tempt
The sailors most sweetly from dismal cliffs; nor Philomela's

Groaning complaint, her lopped murmur, to her cruel sister:
Bards know these things too well. Who by the grave has not
Recounted all the Heliads' boughs and their wept buds;
And Phrygian flint; and him who ventured against Apollo,
When Pallas rejoiced that the boxwood flute deceived his trust?

Let Pity, that has forgotten man, and Justice, recalled
To heaven, and Eloquence in twofold language lament,
And Pallas, and learned Apollo's Pierian escorts;
Those who draw out their epic verse in six-feet metre;
And those who find their toil and renown in the lyre,
Their lot in Arcadian tortoise-shell; and those world-wide
Whom arduous Wisdom numbers in sevenfold fame;
Who have in awful buskins thundered the frenzies of kings,
And stars in the firmament turning their backs on our homes;
And those who gladly fine down their force with pleasant Thalia,
Or dock one pace from their heroic course.
For your creative mind comprehended all wherever
The force of utterance opens the way, whether liking to bind
Its works in the Muses' measures or broadcast prose set loose
In emulation of storms' unbridled rhetoric.

Reveal your face that was suddenly half-obliterate
With dust, Parthenope, lay your hair a volcano's blast
Once buried, on your great foster-son's burial mound;
Than whom neither Athens' fortress nor learned Cyrene
Nor valiant Sparta bore anyone more excelling.
If you had sprung from obscure stock, and lacked renown
Or good family, his citizenship would prove
You Greek and descended from Euboea by ancestral blood.

Each time he celebrated in praiseworthy verse
The Augustalia, he bent his head to you to receive the laurels,
Surpassing the speech of ancient Nestor and that of king
Ulysses, and binding his hair in the semblance of both.

Yours was no degraded birth of obscure blood, your line
Was not inglorious, though expenses had straitened
Your parents' fortune: rich was the ceremony when Childhood
Enjoined your laying aside the proud-worn gold on your
    breast
And the purple-edged toga given to honour your birth.
Straightway at your entry the Muses favourably smiled,
And Apollo, even then inclined to me, dipped your small
Tortoise-shell lyre and steeped your mouth in the holy stream.
Nor is your fatherland's honour single, your place of birth
Depends on uncertain contest between two regions. Hyele,
Acquired by Latian settlers, where the helmsman
Heavy with sleep fell from the poop and kept
His wretched vigil amidst the waves, claims you by clan;
But then the great Parthenope proves you hers by your life's
Long course: thus different cities with different births
Divide up Homer – and each proves right: yet he is not
Truly of either – a huge vainglory puffs up the vanquished.

And there where you commenced your years and greeted life,
You were straightway rushed to local contests, where grown
    men
Could hardly compete, so hot for praise, so bold of wit
Were you. The Euboean masses were stunned at your
Precocious song, and parents showed you to their sons.

Since then you have often contended and never lacked glory
In holy rites: less often green Therapnae applauded
Castor's success in riding, his brother's in boxing.
You won with ease at home. What prowess then to earn
Greek prizes, shading your temples now with Pythian laurel,
And now with Nemean parsley, and now with Isthmian pine,
When Victory, herself each time fatigued as though by age,
Never stole away your wreaths, or touched another's hair!

Hence parents trusted their hopes to you, and noble youths
Were ruled by your teaching and learned the customs and deeds
Of men of old: the fall of Troy; Ulysses' delay;
The power of Homer to rehearse swiftly in verse
The horses and fights of heroes; how Hesiod and Epicharmus
Enriched the godly countryfolk; by what system
Proceeds the flexile voice of Pindar's lyre; Ibycus,
Beseecher of birds; Alcman, performed by sombre Amyclae;
Warlike Stesichorus; heedless Sappho, who was not cowed
By Leucas, but undertook the heroic leap; all others
The lyre finds worthy. Yours the skill to expound
Callimachus' poems, crabbed Lycophron's hidden dens,
Intricate Sophron, and subtle Corinna's arcana.
But why do I speak of trifles? You were accustomed to bear
A yoke equal to Homer's, to match in prose his hexameters
And never to be outdistanced or outpaced.
What wonder they left their countries to seek you out:
Those whom Lucania sent; whom stern Daunia's furlongs;
Whom the homeland mourned by Venus, and region
Passed over by Hercules; whom the virgin sent
Who surveyed from Sorrento's heights the Tyrrhenian sea;

Whom the hill, known from Misenus' trumpet and oar,
By the nearer bay; whom Cyme, once long ago a stranger
To Ausonian household gods; and whom the gulf of
    Dicharchus
And shores of Baiae, where fire gasps intermixed amidst
Deep waters and smothered combustion preserves its lairs?
So, from all sides, peoples came to Avernus' crags,
To the Sibyl's murky cave, to inquire; and she would chant
Concerning the menaces of gods, the deeds of the Fates –
No vain prophet, although she played Apollo false.

And soon you train up Romulus' stock, our future chiefs,
And steadfastly lead them in their forefathers' tracks.
The Vestal torch's Dardanian pontiff throve
Under you, who hides the arcana of what Diomedes stole,
Who learned from you the rite as a boy; you approved Mars'
    priests
And taught them the use of arms, and showed the augurs
The pure air of true prediction; and you may explicate
Cumae's oracle, why the hair of Phrygian priests is covered –
The girded-up Luperci greatly dreaded your blows!

And now of that company one perhaps administers law
To Eastern peoples, another restrains Iberian tribes,
Another at Zeugma contains the Achaemenian Persians.
These curb rich Asiatic populations, those Pontus,
These with peaceable authority perfect the courts, and those
Keep our camps with loyal firmness: you are the source
Of their renown. Neither Nestor nor Phoenix, his untamed
Foster-son's mentor, nor Chiron, who broke with different lore

Achilles' longing to hear the piercing trumpets and horns,
Would have contended with you in forming young men's spirits.

While you were busy thus, civil frenzy suddenly
Waved her torch upon the Tarpeian heights in Phlegraean
Fighting. The Capitol glows with sacrilegious brands,
And native Latian cohorts put on the fury of Gauls.
The flames had barely died down, nor that funeral pyre of gods
Subsided, when you, indefatigable, much swifter
Than the fires themselves, bitterly mourned with religious voice
The thunderbolts captured, gave solace for temples ruined.
The Roman chiefs' and the gods' avenger, Caesar, marvelled;
And amidst the burning, the gods' father, Jupiter, assented.
And lately you had it in mind to mourn in religious chant
Vesuvius' eruption, spending groans for our homeland's damage,
When Jupiter lifted the uprooted mountain from earth
To the stars and hurled it at large on the hapless cities.

Me too, when I attempted the groves of song
And Boeotian vales, when I spoke of my descent from you,
The goddess admitted; for it was not only the stars, the ocean
And lands you gave me, as by custom parents should,
But the lyre's glory, and you first taught me to speak
Unlike the people, and to hope for renown in my tomb.
What was your happiness when with my verse I gladdened
The Roman elders and you were a present witness of your own
Generosity! What confusion, alas, of joy with weeping,
Of a father's hopes and fears with modest rejoicing!
Indeed that day was yours, mine was not the greater glory!
Such is he who watches his youthful son in Olympic lists –
He smites harder, is struck more deeply beneath

His heart, it is more *him* the audience attend, and *him*
The Achaeans watch – while his son's eyes are clogged with
   dust,
And he chokes, and prays for death – provided the prize is
   won!
Alas for me that I bore on my brow only Alban leaves,
And only Ceres' wreath of Augustalian corn
Beneath your gaze! Your Trojan land at Alba
Had hardly contained you had you gained through me
A wreath presented by Caesar! What oaken vigour
Could such a day have given, and how relieved your age!
But mingled oak and olive leaves did not bind my head,
The honour hoped-for fled me. How mildly you accepted
Jupiter's envious verdict! With you as my tutor, my *Thebaid*
Pressed hard the examples set by the classic bards;
You showed me how to spur on my chant, rehearse
The deeds of heroes, the modes of war and the setting
Of scenes. My path wanders within uncertain limits
Without you, my bereaved ship's sails are shrouded in mist.

Your ample familial love cherished not only me:
You were thus as husband too. You knew just one
Marriage-torch, one love. I cannot indeed disjoin my mother
From your pyre now cold: she feels and possesses you,
She sees you, each dawn and dusk she greets your tomb –
As with factitious fidelity other women cultivate
Dolour for Attis and Osiris, and wail over alien graves.

Why should I describe your open but serious manner,
Your good faith, disdain of gold, your care for honour,
Love of truth; or again, when pleased to relax, how pleasant

Your conversation, your understanding that never aged?
For these merits, the gods' just providence has granted you
Renown and bounteous praise, no harsh reverse.

You were taken from us, father, in neither exiguous
Nor superfluous age, having threescore years and five –
But grief and loyalty will not let me enumerate thus,
O father, worthy to pass the bounds of Nestor's age
And equal Prism's seniority, and likewise to see
Me too as old. But Death's door was not harsh for you:
Your case was easy, no lingering egress consigned
Your frame to the waiting tomb in senile decay,
But a dull torpor, and death that mimicked rest
Set you free, and bore you in counterfeit sleep to Tartarus.
How then I groaned – my band of friends saw with concern –
My mother saw, was relieved to recognize her child –
What lamentations I made! Forgive and indulge me, shades:
The truth is, father, *you* would have done as much for *me*.

Happy he who embraced his father with empty arms:
He would have liked to carry him off, though lodged
In Elysium, to bear him a second time through Grecian murk;
And when he strove with living steps to attempt
Tartarus, Hecate's ancient priestess conducted him down.
A lesser cause sent Orpheus' lyre to numbing Avernus;
Thus had Hercules wrought for Alcestis, Admetus' queen.
If one day brought back the shade of Protesilaus, why,
Father, should your lyre, or mine, obtain by prayer
Nothing? Let it be lawful to touch my father's face,
Join hands – and then may come full rigour of any law!

But you, kings of the dead, and Ennean Juno,
Since I pray to and laud you, call off the torch-bearing
Snake-haired Furies; let the gate-guard bark with none
Of his mouths, let sequestered vales conceal the Centaurs
And Hydra's pack and Scylla's abortions, and let
The ultimate Ferryman, the rabble dispersed, invite to the bank
The aged shade, and settle him gently upon the sward.
Go, faithful spirits and troops of Grecian poets,
Scatter Lethean garlands upon his illustrious soul;
Point out the grove, where no Fury intrudes, in which
Is a seeming day and the air is most like that of heaven.
Thence may you come where the better horn subdues
The malignant ivory, and in dreamed pictures teach me,
As you were used to do. So the nymph ordained for Numa,
In the Arician cavern, the holy rites to be observed;
And so, the Ausonians believe, Scipio breathed in dreams
Filled full with Latian Jove; and Sulla too, with Apollo.

[B. S.]

TO SLEEP

Young Sleep, most gentle of gods, by what misdeed
Or mistake have I sadly deserved that I alone
Should lack your gifts? All flocks, wild beasts and birds
Are still; billowing tree-tops evoke reclining rest;
Turbid streams to not resound as they did; turbulent
Waters subside, the sea leans on the land, is quiet.
Seven times now the returning moon has seen my sick
Eyes staring; each time the evening and morning stars
Have revisited me, Aurora has passed by me beseeching,
And pitied, and sprinkled me with dew from her cool whip.
Can I endure? – not if the thousand eyes were mine
Which priestly Argus kept on alternating watches
And never had to stay awake in *all* his body!
If anyone holds his mistress in his twining arms
Throughout the night, and willingly rejects you, Sleep,
Then come – I don't demand that you bury and drown my eyes
With the force of your wings – the happier crowd may pray
For that; touch me with your rod's extremest tip,
Or cross me lightly on hovering feet, it is enough.

[B. S.]

SOMNUS

By what crime or fault of mine have I deserved
To be the only soul without the benefit
Afforded others by this placid baby God?
Settled are the livestock, and the wild as well,
Birds also, for each drooping treetop testifies
To a breezeless slumber; even waterfalls
Recede into the distance as the hackles on
The waves are stroked to smoothness and the sea itself
Lies dormant in the snug of coastal cleavages.
This is the seventh time the moon has swung around
To gaze into my unrelieved returning stare:
As often have the stars of dusk and dawn been back
To peep at me, and, as I toss, Tithonia,
Who drives the twinkling flock before her, sprinkles me
With dewdrops from her whip. So hard to bear!
And how much longer must I? If I had the thousand
Eyes of Juno's watchman I would get at least
More sleep than this – there always was a part of him
Which took a nap. But goodness, now, if anywhere
Some person trammelled in his girl's responding arms
The long night through would drive you off deliberately,
Come here to me, dear Somnus. Not that I insist
That these poor orbs receive a thorough powdering
Of soporific dust dispensed by fluttering –
Happier mortals may demand such luxury!
Simply brush me with your long antenna's tip,
Or tiptoe lightly over me with your hovering step.

[A. H.]

89

Appendix

Statius's poem on insomnia has had many admirers. The finest
tribute is perhaps the sonnet by Drummond of Hawthornden
which serves as our prefatory verse – clearly inspired by *Silvae*
V. 4. We here append John Potenger's early eighteenth-century
translation and a mid-twentieth-century version by the American
poet J. V. Cunningham. But it seems right that Statius himself
should have the last word, and so we conclude this homage to the
poet with his original Latin.

A TRANSLATION OUT OF STATIUS. TO SLEEP

What horrid crime did gentle Sleep displease?
That he refuses me the common Ease
Of Bird and Beast. Nay, every bending Tree
Seems but to nod with Sleep to waking me.
Fierce Rivers softly glide, Seas faintly roar,
And roll themselves asleep upon the Shore.
Seven times the Moon has measured out the Night,
Seven times my Eyes outwatch'd her borrowed light
The shining Stars, as in their Orbs they move,
As oft have seen me waking from above.
Still my Complaints reviv'd Aurora hears,
And mov'd with Pity, baths me in her Tears.
How will my Strength to bear my Grief suffice?
Like Argus I have not a thousand Eyes,
That may alternately their Watching take,
His Body never was all o're awake.
If any amorous youth kind Sleep denies
To lodge, at present, in his wanton Eyes
Clasping with longing Arms the yielding Dame,
And quits his Rest to ease a restless Flame;
Let the ill-treated God take wing to me,
Who have so long beg'd for his Company.
I will not ask him a whole Night to stay;
A happier man must for that Blessing pray;
Let him but call upon me on his way.

JOHN POTENGER
c. 1700

SILUAE 5.4: ON SLEEP

What was my crime, youthful most gentle god,
What folly was it that I alone should lack,
Sweet Sleep, thy gifts? All herds, birds, beasts are still,
The curved mountains seem wearily asleep,
Streams rage with muted noise, the sea-wave falls,
And the still-nodding deep rests on the shore.
Seven times now returning Phoebe sees
My sick eyes stare, and so the morning star
And evening, so Tithonia glides by
My tears, sprinkling sad dew from her cool whip.
How, then, may I endure? Not though were mine
The thousand eyes wherewith good Argus kept
But shifting watch, nor all his flesh awake.
But now, alas! If this long night some lover
In his girl's arms should willingly repel thee,
Thence come sweet Sleep! Nor with all thy power
Pour through my eyes – so may they ask, the many,
More happy –; touch me with thy wand's last tip,
Enough, or lightly pass with hovering step.

J. V. CUNNINGHAM
c. 1950

Crimine quo merui, iuvenis placidissime divum,
quove errore miser, donis ut solus egerem,
Somne, tuis ? tacet omne pecus volucresque feraeque
et simulant fessos curvata cacumina somnos,
nee trucibus fluviis idem sonus; occidit horror
aequoris, et terris maria adclinata quiescunt.
septima iam rediens Phoebe mini respicit aegras
stare genas; totidem Oetaeae Paphiaeque revisunt
lampades et totiens nostros Tithonia questus
praeterit et gelido spargit miserata flagello.
unde ego sufficiam? non si mihi lumina mille,
quae sacer alterna tantum statione tenebat
Argus et haud umquam vigilabat corpore toto.
at nunc heu! si aliquis longa sub nocte puellae
brachia nexa tenens ultro te, Somne, repellit,
inde veni nee te totas infundere pennas
luminibus compello meis – hoc turba precetur
laetior –: extreme me tange cacumine virgae,
sufficit, aut leviter suspense poplite transi.

PUBLIUS PAPINIUS STATIUS

Anvil Press Poetry

Anvil publishes a wide range of translated
classics, modern and contemporary poets in
translation and original poetry in English.
For information please contact us at

anvil@anvilpresspoetry.com